Little Skill Seekers

1-2-3 DRAW!

SCHOLASTIC

New York • Toronto • London • Auckland • Sydney • New Delhi
Mexico City • Hong Kong • Buenos Aires

Cover Design: Tannaz Fassihi
Cover Illustration: Michael Robertson
Interior Design: Mina Chen
Interior Illustration: Radames Espinoza; Amanda Gulliver; James Graham Hale; Doug Jones

Scholastic Inc., 557 Broadway, New York, NY 10012
ISBN: 978-1-338-30635-4
Copyright © Scholastic Inc. All rights reserved. Printed in the U.S.A.
First printing, March 2019.

2 3 4 5 6 7 8 9 10   40   24 23 22 21 20

Dear Parent,

Welcome to *Little Skill Seekers: 1–2–3 Draw*! This fun workbook will help boost confidence and inspire creativity while your child practices fine-motor skills and hand-eye coordination.

Help your little skill seeker build a strong foundation for learning by choosing more books in the Little Skill Seekers series. The exciting and colorful workbooks in the series are designed to set your child on the path to success. Each book targets essential skills important to your child's development.

Here are some key features of *Little Skill Seekers: 1–2–3 Draw*! and the other workbooks in this series:

- Filled with colorful illustrations that make learning fun and playful

- Provides plenty of opportunity to practice essential skills

- Builds independence as children work through the pages on their own, at their own pace

- Comes in a perfect size that fits easily in a backpack for practice on the go

Now let's get started on this journey to help your child become a successful, lifelong learner!

—The Editors

Draw a balloon! Follow the steps in the pictures.

© Scholastic Inc.

Draw more balloons. Then color the picture.

Draw an apple! Follow the steps in the pictures.

Draw more apples. Then color the picture.

Draw a rabbit! Follow the steps in the pictures.

1

2

3

4

5

6

Draw more rabbits. Then color the picture.

Draw a flower! Follow the steps in the pictures.

Draw more flowers. Then color the picture.

Draw a kite! Follow the steps in the pictures.

1

2

3

4

5

6

Draw more kites. Then color the picture.

Draw an owl! Follow the steps in the pictures.

1

2

3

4

5

6

Draw more owls. Then color the picture.

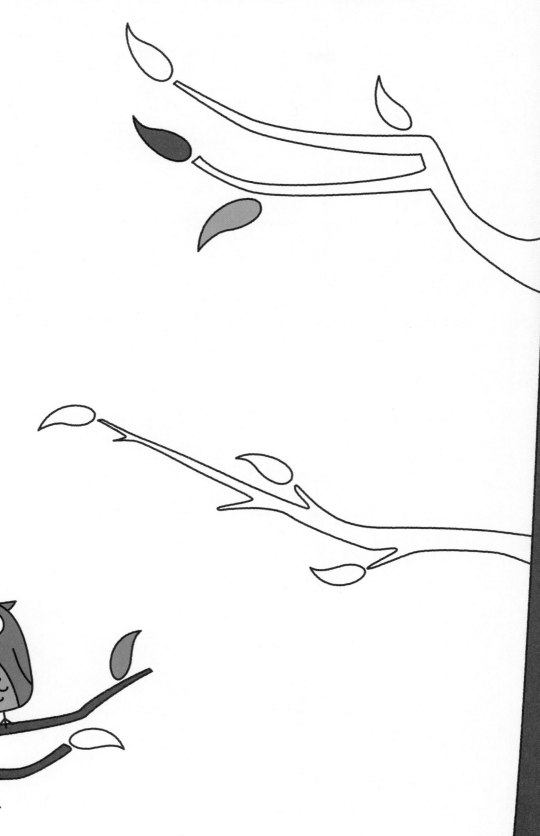

Draw an umbrella! Follow the steps in the pictures.

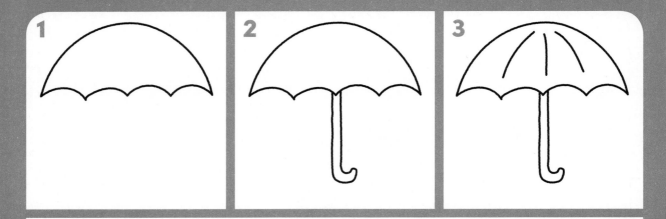

Draw another umbrella. Then color the picture.

Draw a submarine! Follow the steps in the pictures.

Draw more submarines. Then color the picture.

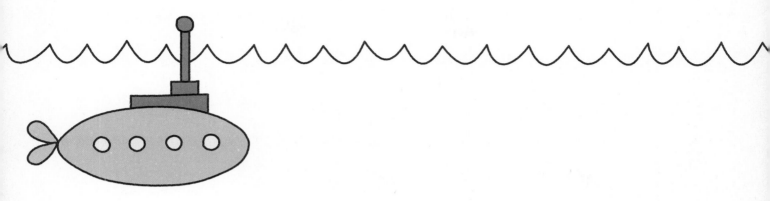

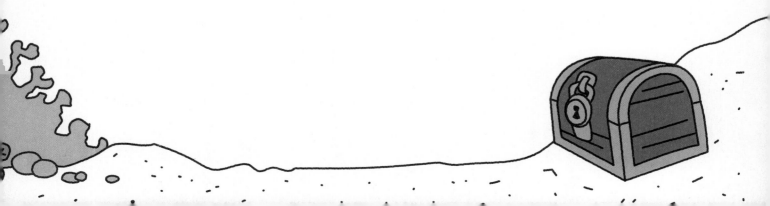

Draw a frog! Follow the steps in the pictures.

Draw more frogs. Then color the picture.

Draw a car! Follow the steps in the pictures.

Draw more cars. Then color the picture.

Draw a penguin! Follow the steps in the pictures.

1

2

3

4

5

6

Draw more penguins. Then color the picture.

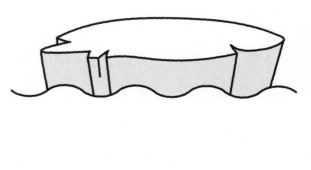

Draw a truck! Follow the steps in the pictures.

Draw more trucks. Then color the picture.

Draw a monster! Follow the steps in the pictures.

Draw more monsters. Then color the picture.

Draw a rocketship! Follow the steps in the pictures.

1

2

3

4

5

6

Draw more rocketships. Then color the picture.

Draw a turtle! Follow the steps in the pictures.

1

2

3

4

5

6

Draw more turtles. Then color the picture.

Draw a fish! Follow the steps in the pictures.

Draw more fish. Then color the picture.

Draw a spaceship! Follow the steps in the pictures.

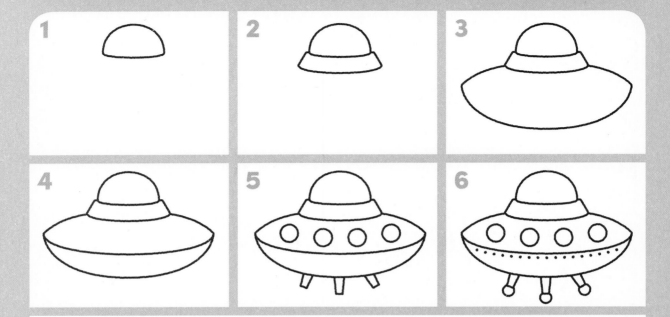

Draw more spaceships. Then color the picture.

Draw a cat! Follow the steps in the pictures.

© Scholastic Inc.

Draw more cats. Then color the picture.

Draw a crab! Follow the steps in the pictures.

Draw more crabs. Then color the picture.

Draw a robot! Follow the steps in the pictures.

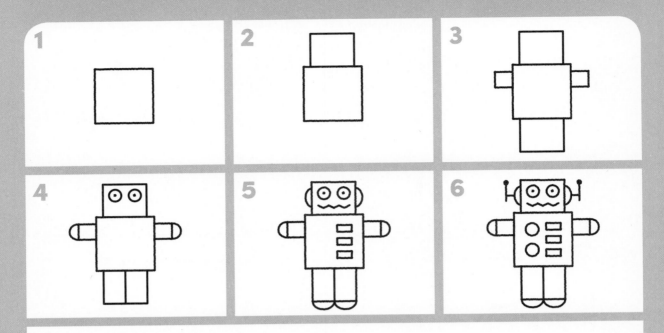

Draw more robots. Then color the picture.

Draw a house! Follow the steps in the pictures.

Draw another house. Then color the picture.

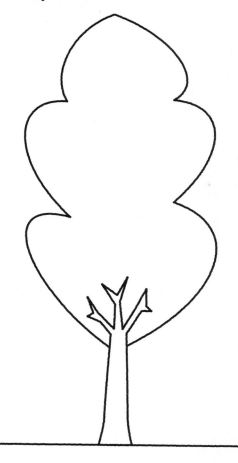

Draw anything you want! Show the steps.

1

2

3

4

5

6

CONGRATULATIONS!

This certificate is awarded to

_____

FOR OUTSTANDING ACHIEVEMENT

_____

Signed

_____

Date